100

tips to be

Happy Together

100

tips to be

Happy Together

Wendy Bristow

BARRON'S

First English edition for North America published by
Barron's Educational Series, Inc., 2004.

First published by **MQ Publications Limited**
12 The Ivories, 6-8 Northampton Street, London, England
website: www.mqpublications.com

Copyright © MQ Publications Limited 2004
Text copyright © Wendy Bristow 2004
illustration: Lucy Truman

Editor: Abi Rowsell
Design: Bet Ayer

All inquiries should be addressed to:
Barron's Educational Series, Inc.
250 Wireless Boulevard
Hauppauge, New York 11788
http://www.barronseduc.com

International Standard Book No. 0-7641-5726-4

Library of Congress Catalog Card No. 2003110642

Printed and bound in China

9 8 7 6 5 4 3 2 1

Contents

Introduction

Boy meets girl . . . they fall in love . . . and live happily after . . . .

Except the stories concentrate on the easy part and tell us nothing about
the difficult stuff. Just how does a loving couple live happily ever after?
How do they keep their love alive on bad days when the in-laws are
staying, the dishwasher's broken, and the baby's got colic? How do they
keep on smiling when money's tight and jobs are being threatened? How
do they weather the storms, resist the temptations, and keep on desiring
each other when they know each other's bodies—and psyches—like
they know their own?

The answer is, with a lot of effort, bucketfuls of goodwill, willingness, and
love. And, as with anything, there are things that help and things that don't;
ways of talking that bring you together and ways that make the gulf between

you wider. There are simple things you can do that make a world of difference. And there are things you do every day that aren't helping. But we're not taught these things at school, so where are we going to learn them?

That's where this book comes in. Packed with hints and tips that have been tried and tested in the real world, it brings the best of expert knowledge, research studies, and what we know that works in the wonderful world of relationships.

If you want your love to last and grow, to meet all your expectations and more, resist the temptations, and bust through the bad days, this is the book for you. A great relationship is a source of joy. Here's how to make it a joy forever. Enjoy!

Remember to Say Hi!

1

Vive la différence!

Until cloning is standard, no two human beings will be exactly alike. So when two individuals get together and decide to entwine their lives, they are bound to come up against differences. Such as: He's a party animal and invites friends over all the time, but she can tolerate only so much human contact before she needs to crawl into a corner with a book. Or she needs clean sheets every day but he could sleep in a pit. But differences are just that—differences. It doesn't mean one's right and the other's wrong. Or one's stupid and the other has the key to the domestic universe. There's a magic key to living with your differences— communication. If you can talk about your likes and dislikes, your wants and needs, you can understand them and work with them, not against them.

2

Think before you speak

Something that helps enormously in any relationship is the art of reflecting; that is, reflecting on your behavior and pondering your other half's. People who don't or won't reflect stand little chance of changing their automatic patterns of relating and virtually no chance of improving relationship glitches. Reflecting means thinking about what you do and why you do it, and the first rule of reflection is to take responsibility for the way you are, rather than blaming everything that might be wrong on the other person. Blame keeps us stuck—and robs us of the possibility of change. Once you're aware of what you're doing, how you're behaving, you can choose to make changes if you like. But if you're not aware, you're on autopilot and nothing will ever alter.

3

Speak up!

Think about the plots in TV soap operas. Half of them wouldn't happen if couples would only tell each other things. You know the kind of scenario:

> "I made a mistake on the household accounts and we've run out of money. And now the man at the newsstand wants to sleep with me and is threatening that if I don't, he'll tell you we're late in paying."

It might all be very entertaining on TV, but in real life, living a soap opera life is exhausting.

When we withhold crucial information, it's because we're afraid: "She won't love me any more if she knows I've made a mistake and am, therefore, (God forbid) not perfect."

"Love is educating the other person as to who you are," says psychotherapist Stanley Keleman. Intimacy works both ways, and you're never going to be loved for your real imperfect self if you're holding something back.

If you recognize that you are withholding, try releasing tiny, not-very-crucial pieces of information first and see how your beloved reacts. If you think your partner is the one holding back, don't nag; use lots of reassurance and lead by example, as in "I want to share a secret with you that I'm embarrassed about." Hopefully, your partner will reciprocate. If not, OK, nag!

4

Sack the private eye

Don't expect your partner to play detective. The "if you loved me, you'd understand me without my having to tell you what's going on" trap is just that—a trap. It's a game anxious people play to test their partners. But partners get confused, angry, or just plain bored with it.

5

Sweat the big stuff up-front

Do discuss the big subjects like marriage, children, and money. It's amazing how many couples go into marriage without ever having had a serious discussion about children: Do we want them? How many? When? How will we bring them up? And then they wonder why they have different views AFTER marriage.

6

Ch-ch-ch-ch-changes

Know that you can never change another person. You can, however, change your own behavior, and when you do, the dynamics alter. Say it drives you nuts that he is always complaining about his mother but never to her face. Next time he starts whining, tell him, "I'm not going to listen. You know my views on the subject." Left to stew in his own juice, all the evidence says he is more likely to say something to her. Either way, you don't have to listen to hours of moaning about her.

Detaching—taking the focus off trying to change your partner and working at your own options for living with the situation—always improves things. Eventually. It may seem strange at first.

7

What does love mean to you?

For such a small word it's an enormous concept and means very
different things to different people. When my parents argued, my father
would always say, "But I never go for a drink like other men." That was
evidently how he was showing my mother his love. But I'm not
convinced "not going for a drink" was what she saw as love. She
wanted romance. She wanted appreciation.

A fun way to play with the concept of love is to each make a list of
caring behaviors, as in, "When you do so-and-so, I feel loved." It might
be things like cooking dinner, or simply saying "I love you," or surprising
your partner with presents or, if you must, not going for a drink. Pin your
list on the kitchen wall and you won't have misunderstandings—or any
excuse for forgetting!

8

Your love account

One of the power tools in your relationship toolbox is appreciation. And compliments. It's so easy to take our partners for granted and not appreciate them for what they do. It's not difficult to say, "It was great the way you handled that angry driver this morning," or "I really appreciate your taking out the garbage this week." It's like making payments into your love account.

9

Five to one

Top marriage guru John Gottman, in his groundbreaking research on happy couples, discovered what he calls the "magic ratio" of 5 to 1. "As long as there is five times as much positive feeling and interaction between husband and wife as there is negative," he says, "we found the marriage was likely to be stable." So, on a bad day, make sure you make up for any negative feelings with.plenty of positivity and love.

10

Get specific

Whether we're talking about nice stuff or, as we'll see later, nasty stuff, what works best in all communication is being specific. If your honey says, "You always look nice," it's good. But it's not half as powerful as, "When you put on your blue suit and comb your hair back, you look so fabulous I just want to run down the road after you."

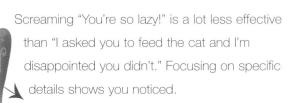

Screaming "You're so lazy!" is a lot less effective than "I asked you to feed the cat and I'm disappointed you didn't." Focusing on specific details shows you noticed.

11

Take out the bad words

While you're at it, eliminate the words "always" and "never" from your vocabulary and throw out "should" and "ought." It's hard to utter any of these words without sounding like a nag. "You never put your pants in the laundry hamper" is probably not strictly true and will only encourage your other half to be specific about the one time he did put his pants there. You may also get hackles rising with, "You should have taken out the trash." "Can you take out the trash?" could elicit wise-ass replies like "Well, I *could* . . . ." So it's best to say, "I'd like you to take out the trash." In the area of psychology known as "transactional analysis," the "You should have . . ." part of the sentence is known as "critical parent" words. They make you sound superior and always bring out the worst in the person they're directed at.

12

Are you listening?

One of the greatest gifts you can give is
to listen well; that is, listen without
interrupting, without making remarks
like "Well, what the hell did you do
that for?" and without gazing at the
TV screen just to the left of your
sweetheart's ear. When one of you
needs to talk, turn that TV off!
Especially if your sweetheart is stressed
and is talking to let off steam, the best way to listen
is to make eye contact, nod sympathetically, and
offer the occasional "Oh, dear."

13

Button that lip

One of the best ways to mess up the admirable art of listening is to listen and then offer solutions. Both sexes hate solutions, for different reasons. Women hate them because, when stressed, they talk to let off steam, and all they want to hear is an occasional "Oh, dear." Men hate them because, if a woman tells a man what he should have done or offers other advice, he immediately feels like a failure and wants to go drink alone in a bar.

The battle of the sexes wouldn't be half so combative and many an unhappy marriage would perk up if men would only shut up with the solutions. The trouble is, men are programmed to offer solutions. If a woman is stressed and pouring out her heart, her man wants to fix it. So to fix it, he offers solutions. For a woman, just talking makes her feel better, and solutions take up her needed talking time.

14

Men do talk less than women

Whether it's because they're from Mars or because they're basically hunters programed to stare at the horizon for hours figuring out where the next meal is going to leap from, men really do have times when they quit talking and ruminate until they've worked out the solution to their problems. This is another reason men hate advice from women. They need to figure it out for themselves or they don't feel like men. The best thing a man's partner can do is wait it out until he perks up and chats again. The worst thing a man's partner can do is ask, "Why won't you *talk* to me?"

15

Love means . . .

Apologies to all the romantics out there who wept a whole Kleenex box during *Love Story*, but love *does* mean saying you're sorry—in the real world. We often get caught up in thinking, "I'm not going to apologize first; it was her stupid fault; she's the one in the wrong." But sometimes a simple apology melts all the hurt and hostility and opens up the possibility of escaping the who's right trap. Then you can start to really get somewhere. If you aren't the one in the wrong, it can be especially powerful.

16

Be nice!

How was your day? How are you feeling? How was work? How were the kids? These are the baseline niceties of living with someone. Unfortunately, with familiarity and years of living with the contents of someone else's underwear drawer, they can fly right out the window. Trivia is of the essence.

17

I notice that . . .

A powerful technique to help you button your lip is to use the phrase, "I notice . . ." As in, "I notice you're really upset about this." Or, "I notice you don't want to talk about this." It's a way of affirming your partner, it shows you're listening, it displays empathy, and it's neutral. Even if your partner is feeling depressed and is spending all weekend in the recliner watching TV, "I notice that you're spending all weekend watching TV" is a lot nicer than "Get the hell outta the recliner!"

18

Timing is also of the essence

It might sound like common sense, but it's amazing how often this basic rule can be broken. Pick your moments carefully to talk about the big stuff. Don't bring up the topic of why his mother doesn't like you when he's negotiating a nasty bend in the road in a foreign country. It might be a fine moment for you, but you're not thinking of him and, frankly, you're asking for a fight. It's a good idea to schedule big conversations by mutual agreement. As in, "Can we talk about your mother this weekend? Maybe on Saturday after you get back from the game? OK, if not then, when?"

19

Don't assume

One of the biggest mistakes we make in any communication, whether with our partner or our assistant who got the sandwich order wrong, is to assume. There's a tacky saying that goes, "ASSUME makes an ASS of U and ME!" And it's right. It's better to ask lots of questions than to make lots of assumptions. Remember that assumptions easily turn into accusations and certainly create misunderstandings.

20

No-nos

Sarcasm, interrupting, or belittling your partner (especially in public or in private), shouting, and, obviously, any form of violence are most definitely out if you want to live happily ever after.

21

Praise your partner

Say that your partner is telling you how she did at work today. What do you do? Do you pick on every little thing she did wrong, or do you praise her? Partners puff up like a lion at the words, "It sounds like you handled that really well." And they deflate like a popped balloon at the first sign of criticism. Remember, you're the most important person in your partner's world. You have the power to make your partner feel like a million dollars or not worth a dime. Use that power wisely.

22

Stay in neutral

One trick for minimizing communication glitches is to keep your language neutral. And the easiest way to do that is to make liberal use of the word "I" and be stingy with the word "you." "I'm tired tonight" is a lot more useful than "What would you like to do tonight?" "I would like that wall painted" is much better than, "You should paint that wall." Using "I" opens up options and gives the other person choices (maybe he thinks the wall is just fine). "You" closes them and paves the way for conflict. "I" also helps you take responsibility for your half of the relationship. Always a good thing. Just try it and see.

23

Three little words

"I love you" are words no one ever gets tired of hearing. The words that should be the last word in any argument. You know what they are. Say them.

24

Watch their behavior

For all we've said about communication, it really is true that actions speak louder than words. So he keeps saying he'll paint the bathroom, but years later, it's still that icky green. So she keeps saying she'll marry you, but she's never worn the ring you gave her. Some people spend years waiting for that magic thing their partner says she'll do. If you think she's procrastinating, say so. It's good to talk, but if nothing ever gets done, the words don't mean diddly-squat.

R-E-S-P-E-C-T

Does your partner criticize you in public? Does he say things in private that you'd never put up with from someone else? What are you, a doormat? If he says things that are unacceptable, make it clear you're not standing for it. Criticism works on a relationship like rust on a car. It erodes love and trust and all those good things until the whole thing falls apart. And you don't want that.

Taking Out the Garbage

26

Creative compromise

As we said in the last chapter, no two people can be entirely the same domestically, sexually, socially, or practically. He does everything slowly; she does it all like a bat out of hell. He's a maniac with the Dust-buster; she makes Mr. and Mrs. Slob look positively neat. Those differences are part of what attracted you in the first place. And we've established that the one you love is probably not going to change from a messy soul to a cleaning demon, so you need to find some way of living with it and meeting in the middle.

27

What do you expect?

The source of many, if not most problems between couples is a clash of expectations around practicalities like money, housework, and sex—how much, how often, how well we do it. And the trouble with expectations is that they're usually unconscious and go so deep that we believe in them with a fanaticism approaching the religious. Couples somehow expect that their sweeties will automatically understand just HOW MUCH it means that you wipe the sink after you've washed up. But it ain't necessarily so. Become a private detective investigating your own—and your partner's—relationship expectations. What you expect—and why—is usually fascinating and will help to bring couples closer together.

28

Divvy-up the drudgery

Tasks you both hate? Make a list, agree which are equivalent—for example, taking out the garbage is as nasty as cleaning the bathroom, doing the dusting is just as boring as weeding the garden—and divide them up. Include all your household chores from gardening to laundry to cleaning to dusting to child care to feeding the cat to buying and preparing the food and paying the bills. Now divide up the tasks and make an agreement to stick to this regimen for a fixed amount of time. No, it isn't very romantic, but whereas falling in love "just happens," housework doesn't.

When the agreed-upon period is up, review the regimen and see how it's working. Know you can always change the contracts if they don't seem fair or they're more than you can manage—or you just want a change. If there's a shift in the workload—you have a baby, one of you gets laid off—you'll have to renegotiate.

29

Barter your energies

See housework, child care, and money as forms of energy. If one of you is prepared to fork out the energy of money as a replacement for using the energy of brainpower or horsepower, so be it. Money buys time and energy. I know a couple who agreed to actually pay one of them to do the housework. Anything is possible if you both agree. Remember, also, that it doesn't have to be forever. "Let's try this for three months and then review it" is a useful starting point.

30

Hire help

If you've tried divvying-up the chores and it just isn't working—one of
you just hates housework or can't seem to manage the time—hire a
housekeeper or cleaning service. They don't have to come every week.
A good going-over twice a month might keep things on an even keel.
And a relationship isn't worth losing over that ring around the bathtub.

31

For richer, for poorer

Money causes more conflict and creates more divorces than any other
subject, including sex. All the experts agree that a good solution for
coupled-up finances is a joint account for joint business that you both
contribute to and separate accounts for personal uses. That way, she
never gets to see how much you spent on her present, and vice-versa.

Opposites attract

For some peculiar reason best left to science, couples tend to polarize over money. Say that you were a little extravagant and he was quite careful when you met. But a couple of years down the line, you're a compulsive spender and he's Scrooge. Or it's you who's hoarding every penny and he who's showing the neighbors the new Porsche. People get frightened and threatened by their partner's spending habits and try to compensate, so their behavior gets more extreme.

So get real. It's when we do things unconsciously that we get into trouble. But once you realize that your spending (or hoarding) is a response to his spending (or hoarding), you have some choices. The best choice, as ever, is to meet each other halfway.

33

Speaking up for moms

Women really don't want to do all the child care. A fast and very effective way to make a woman fall out of love is for her partner to discount the sheer amount of hard work that goes with being a mother. Yes, there are many times when only Mom will do for an upset child, but Mom will want time off every so often, or she just might go pop. Thankfully, we live in a society where the old structures are breaking down and it's well recognized that a child needs a healthy relationship with both parents. The trouble is, our unconscious expectations and beliefs about child care can defeat that. As long as you keep thinking about what parenting means to you, you stand a good chance of cracking old codes.

34

Draw up a contract

If one of you won't be earning for a while, make a contract. For example, "I will support you and pay for all vacations for five years while we have young children, but after that you'll go back to work and you'll support me while I take that art course I want to take." Be clear about the future, make agreements and you'll prevent anxiety attacks down the line. Big changes always feel threatening. But if each partner knows the deal, there will be fewer arguments later.

35

Look at Mr. Lazy

If you're shirking your responsibilities around the house, ask yourself
what that's about. Are you resentful? Are you angry at your partner and
not saying so and using this as a way to get
revenge? Or does it just plain bother you
so little that you don't even notice when
it's dusty and it's your turn to dust?
Making a housework agreement and
then breaking it is not just letting your
partner down, it's letting yourself
down, too.

36

Play to your strengths

If one of you loves paperwork and the other gets turned on by tidiness, agree that the paper-fiend does all the bills while the tidiness-fiend tidies. We all do our best when doing things we love.

37

Create rewards

Both hate housework? Then create incentives. Agree that if you both clean the house together your reward will be take-out pizza. If you both paint the living room you'll plan a weekend away. Deep down, we're all children and, like kids, we work better with rewards.

38

Money talks

Just as it's important to be clear and specific about chores and who's doing what, it's important to be clear about who's spending what. If money is tight, you might want to agree on a budget. Yes, it's a horrible word, but people work best when they're clear about what they're doing, and being a fool with money is nothing to be proud of. Money can often be harder to talk about than sex, but not discussing it leads to misery if you have opposing spending personalities. And, as with many things, couples do polarize over money—a hoarder hooks up with a spender, and so on. Find that crucial middle ground.

Home sweet home

Talking about how things were done in the home you grew up in can be very revealing. It may be that Mrs. expects Mr. to take out the garbage because that was how it was done at home, without question, so she just expects it. But in his first home, maybe the maid took out the garbage, so he sees it as a demeaning thing to do. We invest great meaning and expectations in the mundane, routine things we do every day. So it's easy to start thinking he's a bad person because he doesn't take out the garbage; we forget that he's just a different person with a different viewpoint.

40

Doing it all

Just as couples polarize over money, they can polarize over chores and over the basic responsibilities of living. A common dynamic is known as overfunctioning and underfunctioning. Here, one partner takes on all the responsibility, arranges the social life, and washes the dishes while the other lazes around eating chocolate. A common trait is that the one doing it all constantly nags at the one not doing it. But if the doing-it-all partner would only let up, the underfunctioning one would probably take up the slack. This dynamic is usually about control—the do-er gets to feel superior and in control, but at the considerable expense of the partner feeling inferior, wrong, and understandably resentful. The do-er needs to stop rescuing and trust his partner to take some responsibility. Miracles do happen!

Come Here and Say That!

41

It's OK to argue

If your parents never argued, it's easy to think you're a terrible person if you let it rip. Or, if your partner lets it rip, it may frighten you very much. But expression of anger, if it's kept within safe boundaries, is just that—expression. It gets it out and over with. It keeps it from simmering away inside and building and building until it explodes in a violent rage, an affair, or someone's walking out—which is what repressed anger has a habit of doing. Unexpressed anger destroys relationships, simple as that. You're actually doing your partner a favor by getting cross. If you handle your anger properly, you'll feel better afterward. Just keep your language neutral!

42

Play to win/win

Aim for a win/win situation, not a win/lose situation. Ask yourselves: What step could we take here so we both win? This will involve generating lots of options, and it may involve negotiations that make the United Nations look like a walk in the park. You could say that lasting love is all about compromise. But who wants to be in a relationship where one partner always wins? You don't have to be psychic to predict that the always-losing partner will one day flip out.

43

It's not a competition

Many people find closeness threatening and see the inevitable clashes of needs and expectations as a competition they must win at all costs. This kind of thing may work fine in the office, but do you really want the cost to be your relationship? Do you really want to trample all over your lover's needs and happiness just to be on top? In other words, do you want to be right, or do you want to be happy?

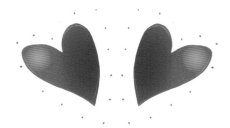

44

Join up for the same team

The trick is to remember that you're both on the same team. That's why you got together. Stop focusing on "you're wrong, I'm right" and think instead about the practical, doable thing that would get both of your needs met. There is always something that can be done.

45

Throw out the kitchen sink

When you're arguing, try to avoid what the Australians call "gunnysacking"—throwing everything in the gunnysack (an enormous piece of luggage for traveling long distances). The phrase that sums up gunnysacking is "and ANOTHER thing . . . ." Try to stick to the matter at hand and don't bring up the fact that last week she came home late and didn't call and the week before that she didn't wash the dishes.

46

Bearing a grudge

We humans are imperfect beings, and if you insist on carrying a grudge about what your sweetheart did three months ago, you're only going to stack up misery for yourself. And for your partner. Forgiveness isn't something that just happens. It's a skill.

47

Below the belt

It helps to agree early in your relationship about the "belt-line issues." That is, those things that, if they happened, would prevent you from continuing in the relationship. These might or might not include infidelity, flirting, violence, and verbal abuse—or squeezing the toothpaste from the wrong end! They can be whatever you make them.

48

Do sweat the small stuff

One way to prevent a grudge from building up is to talk about the little things that bug you in a small way—before they explode in a huge way. Women are brought up to be nice and are especially bad at pointing out things that bother them in a small way because it's NOT nice. But then they explode like the nag from hell and that's definitely not nice.

There's a difference between nagging and saying, "You know what? I'm really annoyed about your coming in late last night and not calling me." And at least he knows where he stands.

49

The key to happiness

The crux to dealing with conflict—and future happiness—is to RESOLVE the anger. All the experts agree that couples get in trouble when they have the same old argument over and over and *nothing ever changes*.

You need to negotiate and agree on a course of action that will ensure the problem won't arise again or that will make you deal with it differently. That's how the problem gets resolved. Stuck? Ask friends for more options.

50

Get help!

If you can't resolve an issue alone, ask friends or a therapist to help. Arguments that happen over and over are often touching some deep feelings or beliefs, and the pair of you may get so stuck, you can't see a way out. Another perspective can save a situation you might think is insoluble.

51

Fight clean

Don't go below the belt and resort to insults. Don't interrupt. Don't belittle or psychoanalyze: "Just because your mother never loved you, don't go cold with me." Stick to the facts.

52

How to complain

Now for the nitty-gritty of fighting. The trick, as we know, is to be really specific. So don't make sweeping complaints: "You never wash the dishes!" But be specific, using the "I" word to keep the focus on you and your response, not on your partner and what a terrible person he is. Say, "I'm angry that you haven't washed the dishes one single evening this week." Then, include the magic ingredient: Explain the *effect* his behavior has on you in specific detail. "When you don't wash the dishes, when we agreed you would if I cooked, I feel like a drudge and I resent you. It makes me not want to have sex with you."

53

Recommendations, please!

Step two. Don't just complain. If you only complain and tell him about the effect on you, that's what's known in the trade as moaning. What makes a difference is being really specific about what you want to see instead. This can take a bit of work because it forces you to take responsibility for what you want rather than the easier route of focusing on how bad he is. "I want you to take out the trash every week, please" is relatively straightforward. But what if you're unhappy that he's not affectionate anymore? What do you want? How many kisses? How many love notes? It sounds silly, but the clearer you are about what you want, the greater the chance you'll get it.

54

Count to ten

So you've made your complaint, you've made your recommendation, but you're still having an argument. And the anger feels overwhelming. Anger can make you say things you may regret forever. ("The sex is lousy" comes to mind.) There are things you can do to catch yourself in time. Counting to ten can help. So can asking for time-out while you calm down. Then doing something physical really helps. Anger is a physical emotion—it literally readies us for fight. So go for a run, exercise vigorously, or punch a cushion.

55

Know your anger style

Knowing how you react to anger is useful. Do you get quiet and fume? Do you explode and say things you regret? Do you get aggressive and attack? All these things are your automatic responses and may not help your relationship in the long run.

56

Don't be defensive

The sum of human misery could be dramatically reduced if people let down their guards and weren't so defensive. Yes, when someone makes a complaint, even if it's done by the book, it can feel like a criticism or an attack. And the common reaction is to heave up onto that high horse and come out with something like, "Whattayamean, I didn't wash the dishes?" Some people will argue that black is white and that they were a veritable human dishwasher rather than admit that, yes, they messed up. But that is very frustrating to the partner, and acting defensive always lessens your chances of getting anywhere.

Try this: The next time you feel attacked and want to defend, just agree, "Yes, I *did* do that." You may just see your sweetie melt.

57

Stick to your guns; don't give in

If an issue is really important to you, stick to your guns or you'll only make yourself unhappy. Giving in creates resentment more effectively than anything. It's a common cause of women losing interest in sex. Unconsciously they think, "OK, he won't vacuum the house for me, I won't have sex for him."

58

But don't be stubborn, either!

Once again, do you want to be right or do you want to be happy?

59

Keeping it in the family

If you find yourself acting really stubborn, getting on your high horse,
feeling resentful, going cold, or throwing plates around, chances are
you're acting like one of your parents.

 Growing up we absorb information, patterns, and role
models for how to be in a relationship from the first
relationship we witness on a day-to-day basis (usually our parents).
Then we automatically and unconsciously behave that way when we're
in a relationship. Which one of your parents are you acting like? And do
you really want your parents' relationship?

60

Be a pair, not a threesome

Keep a united front when you're with other people—the children, your in-laws, friends. Don't let others come between you. What psychologists call "triangling" is to be avoided at all costs. This is taking sides against your partner with your mother, your daughter, or the man who mows the lawn. It's moaning to your mother about your partner and asking her to speak with him. It's asking your partner to deal with his sister when it's you she's offended. Either way, it's involving another person in the intimate business of your relationship. The only other person who should ever get involved is your couples therapist. Or maybe the cat.

Watch out for the velvet glove

Don't get hooked by manipulation. Not all manipulation is out-and-out obvious. There's what's known as "the velvet glove," which operates subtly and covertly. Examples of this might be, "It's only because I love you that I don't want you to go out with your friends without me" or "I know you and I don't think you can do that job." If you feel guilty about doing something or asking for something you believe you have an absolute right to, chances are you're being manipulated. Not sure? Try calling her on it and see what happens.

62

Ding-ding! Round over

Arguing is exhausting. Take time out from talking about difficult subjects. If you're going around and around in circles, agree to take a break and set another time to discuss it further. Often, when you break a deadlock and calm down, you come up with your best ideas about how to solve a problem. Save it for round two.

63

Does it matter profoundly?

One of my friends asks herself, "Does it matter profoundly?" In other words, if he never puts his socks in the laundry hamper ever again, can you live with it? Sometimes you surprise yourself.

64

Take it to the right address

Don't get into the habit of taking your other
frustrations out on your partner. It's tempting
because it's your partner who's closest. But this
behavior is corrosive over time. If the kids have been
acting up all day or your boss has been in a mood, it's plain bad
manners to pick an argument with your spouse just to get the
anger out. Better to go to the gym, walk around the block, or again,
punch a cushion (physical outlets
get anger over with faster) than to
harm your relationship.

65

Goodwill

Experts agree that the magic ingredient, the factor that ensures you'll resolve your conflict (or learn to live with it unresolved), is goodwill. Being defensive, not taking responsibility, taking unrelated things out on your partner—things like this erode goodwill. If you still have goodwill for each other, you'll work it out. It's a sad day, indeed, when the goodwill goes. That's when divorces happen. Research shows that men, in particular, are prone to not taking their partner's complaints seriously. Then, when her goodwill is entirely gone and she calls time, they're astonished. Don't let this happen to you.

Keeping the Romance Alive

66

Don't be a PEA-brain

When we fall in love, a series of chemical reactions go off in our brains. The main chemical released—PEA (phenylethylamine)—gives us that elated feeling and makes us see our beloved in a not-entirely-real way. We put on the rose-tinted glasses, ignoring the imperfections and exaggerating the good stuff. We really are in an altered state—nature's way of conning us into mating with people we might not like otherwise. But the very longest our brains can produce PEA is two years. After it wears off, we see our sweeties more realistically. We see those things we didn't want to see before, and we see them in Technicolor. Sometimes we don't like what we see and try to change it. This begins the phase some couples therapists call the power struggle.

Some people become addicted to the PEA high. They really are love addicts and end a relationship the minute the infatuation goes and the PEA wears off. But the depth of affection, security, and comfort that comes from the attachment phase, the period when you see each other for the real people you truly are and love each other anyway, is worth so much more than the blissed-out state of PEA-brain. Plus, attachment doesn't wear off. Get it right and it only gets deeper.

67

Keep dating

Don't be one of those couples who stop doing the good stuff. A powerful way of reminding yourselves how it felt in the PEA stage is to continue doing the things you did then. Go out for dinner or to the movies once a week. Book a baby-sitter for every Friday night for the foreseeable future and get out of the house. Put these dates on your calendar and stick to them. The couples who date together stay together.

68

Accentuate the positive

If you want to change something in bed, never, ever criticize. If you do, you're hurting your lover at his deepest, most vulnerable place. Say, "Mmm, do that," not "Don't do that!" Focus on what you like, not what you don't like. Moan a little (or a lot) when he does what you like, and move his hand when he does what you don't. If he doesn't get the message and you need to come right out and say it, don't do it in bed. And when you do it, do it tenderly and, again, positively, concentrating on what you like, not on what he does wrong.

69

Get help

If you need help with what goes on between the sheets, see a sex therapist. Problems are common, and there are simple techniques that really work. If it was your car that needed fixing, you'd take it to the garage. Why not you?

70

Slaves to the rhythm

Many sex therapists say problems arise because women have a need-sex rhythm of ten days but men only two to three days. Try not having sex for ten days and see if, then, you can't leave him alone.

Thrills and spills

A powerful way to ensure that you keep things new between you is trying new things together. Keep having adventures that stretch you as a couple and give you new joint experiences that go way beyond the sofa. Vacations together to unusual places, bungee jumping, discovering opera—you can experiment à deux with all those things you've always wondered about doing. It's a great antidote to that "settled-down" feeling. Research shows that couples are prone to falling in love when they're in testing situations—think of all those war-time romances. Getting slightly scared together sparks romance anew.

73

Feed your brain

The largest sexual organ is the brain—send each other saucy e-mails and naughty text messages. Talk about what you'd like to do to each other later to get those sexy synapses snapping. Anticipation is half the thrill—especially for women whose excitement thrives when their brain is involved.

72

Bust that rut

A sexual relationship thrives on novelty and spontaneity—surprise your sweetie with new underwear or by seducing him on the couch. In sex surveys, men's most common complaint is, "She won't try anything new." You might like it, too!

74

Don't go along different lines

When you both lead busy lives, it's easy to fill up your day with work, other people, and family, and have nothing left for your love affair. Love is like a third person in the relationship—if that person is neglected, she'll leave. You need to feed her, spend time with her, nurture her, just as if she were a plant. Couples counselors have identified a type of relationship they call "parallel lines," in which the partners trot along through life together, getting stuff done, but having no real point of connection. It's easy for this type of relationship to become empty and die. And it's one that's especially vulnerable to outside temptation.

The ideal, say the experts, is the "H-frame" relationship, where partners lead independent lives but are connected—by heart, love, sex, but most of all, by *communicating*.

Remember all those nights you sat up talking in the early days? It's easy to reestablish a connection right now by just sharing something meaningful with your partner. Couples who do re-connect after a rut hit a whole new level of romance, like falling in love all over again.

75

Looking good

Men's sexuality is far more visual than women's. If the female partner gets dressed up and flits around the bedroom a little every now and then, the male partner will go ga-ga. The reason so much naughty underwear is black or red is it is the most visually exciting, offering the biggest contrast to white skin. White underwear works equally well if your skin is dark.

76

Fake not

Don't fake pleasure you don't feel—you only leave yourself open to dissatisfaction. Intimacy can't thrive if there's pretense between you.

77

Use it or lose it!

If you get into a no-sex rut, break it! Sexual activity produces the attachment hormone oxytocin in a woman's brain. No-sex couples really do feel more distant. And the more distant you feel, the less you want sex. It becomes a vicious circle. And when you're not having sex with each other, different people become more tempting.

78

Make an effort

One of the best ways to enhance intimacy is by making love when
you don't feel like it, believe it or not! A study at Indiana University's
Kinsey Institute found that having sex when you're feeling low can
foster intimacy. Given that sexual excitement thrives on novelty, it *is*
easy to get in a rut when faced with that same old body. Some
couples, however, find that imposing a sex routine,
such as "Wednesday night is sex night," can reignite
that spark.

79

How good is good?

In the Western world, the percentage of couples who say they have a satisfactory sex life averages out at around 60 percent. So despite the images of five-times-a-night we're bombarded with by movies, magazines, and TV, perfection isn't the norm! On a similar note, the number of women who climax via intercourse alone is 26 percent. If your sexual expectations are sky-high, you might need a reality check.

80

Nature's little joke

Often sexual relationships break down because of a glitch in
nature's programming: a basic difference between the sexes that
causes no end of trouble. Men have sex to feel close, whereas women
need to feel close to have sex.

In studies, women always describe the condition of the relationship—
whether he's been attentive, whether he's washed the dishes—as
affecting whether they feel the heat or not, whereas men see sex
as a way of letting off steam and a way of *being* attentive.

Men report feeling all the things
women want in order to want sex
with them—emotional, loving,
willing—*after* sex.

In an ideal world, the way to get around this glitch is for the man to act attentive anyhow, recognizing that, most of the time, women need to be seduced to feel womanly. And women need to understand that men aren't just "after one thing," that his sexual overtures are about his wanting two things—sex, and the loving, close feelings that come with it.

81

Kiss and cuddle

For couples who have lost their va-va-voom, sex therapists recommend a program of "sensate focus." Here the couples spend a certain time each night stroking, kissing, massaging—but sexual touching or intercourse is banned for a couple of weeks. This brings sensuality back into the relationship, and the pair usually discovers that after two or so weeks of this, they can't keep their hands off each other. It's crucial that you don't lose sensuality in your relationship. Remember the time when you couldn't keep your hands off each other. Massages are a great way to keep it going and unwind at the same time.

82

The two-step

Many experts describe intimacy as a dance. One very common dynamic is that of "seeker and sought," in which one of you does all the chasing and the other likes to be chased. It's a complicated, delicate dynamic designed to create the amount of intimacy that the two of you can manage. Maybe the sought after one distances because he's afraid he'll feel suffocated if the seeker gets too close. In a healthy relationship, we swap roles over the long-term. The seeker gets a busy job and is somewhat distracted, and the sought starts seeking because he misses the intimacy. When you swap these roles, it keeps the romance coming. When you each get stuck in one role forever, the romance dies.

83

Count your blessings

Review the relationship every now and again and see how far you've come. Talk to each other about how you've changed. Often we keep these observations to ourselves, but they can be a great opportunity to give each other a loving pat on the back. Focus on the positive and get a gratitude attitude!

84

Is it a physical thing?

Sometimes a person's libido drops through the floor. It can be caused by emotional factors—depression, anger, or lack of love. But it can also be a symptom of a physical problem. Loss of libido is a symptom of some medical conditions and can have a medical cause. If in doubt, check with your doctor.

85

Trust you

Trust. It's one of the cornerstones of an intimate relationship and nearly impossible to regain once lost. Relationships do survive affairs, but it's deeply painful, risky work, and the guilty party nearly always decides that the moments of excitement the broken trust bought weren't worth the price. One rule of thumb is to never do anything you wouldn't want your partner doing. If you're sharing secret, flirty e-mails with a member of the opposite sex, think about how you would feel if your partner were doing the same thing. If you're flirting outrageously with the boy in accounting, how would it be if you found out he had a similar crush?

An extra-marital attraction is always a symptom of something you want in your core relationship that you're not getting. How might you get it there and save yourself much heartache?

Making it Last Forever

It's possible . . .

. . . that whatever attracted you in the beginning may drive you crazy in the end. I know a man who fell in love partly because his girl was from a huge family and he found her closeness to her clan a big turn-on. Several years later, the fact that family members were always dropping in was driving him crazy. Even if it was her great personality and sense of humor which pulled you in, you may later find her ability to charm, or to make a joke of everything a challenge in some way.

Try to remember what you loved about your partner's childish qualities before, say, you felt like you'd turned into a parent.

87

Could you live with clones?

Ask yourself, Would I want children who were exactly like this person? Experts say it's a good measure of long-lasting love. If the answer is, "Yes," go for it. If not, be aware that there's a good chance it's what you might end up with. If he's a sports freak and you love culture, you might end up the only arty one in a family of sports freaks. If that thought makes you shudder, you need to ask why.

88

Get out of the control tower

Controlling behavior and long-lasting love go together like ice cream and mashed potatoes. Men and women try to be in control in different ways. Women tend to do it around the home; men do it in cars, with money, at work, and with maps. It's good and healthy if the "who's in control" acknowledges the areas that the other is best at controlling. But if one partner is constantly controlled by the other, troubles can arise.

Welcome to the perils of the lean-to relationship, where one partner leans on the other to make all their decisions and the other enjoys being in charge. The danger is that one partner might get tired of being bossed

around and decide to stand on her own two feet. Or the other partner might get tired of the responsibility of controlling and look for a more assertive lover. When the dynamic in the lean-to relationship changes, the relationship tends to collapse.

Remember:

Equality **+** balance **=** good.

Doormats **+** domineering **=** not good.

The trick is to aim for equality and keep love alive. A tiny change in your own behavior today—taking more responsibility for something, or buttoning your lip if you're about to dictate—can reap huge rewards tomorrow.

89

Don't fall into the "if only" trap

If life were perfect, there'd be no traffic jams and pets wouldn't shed on your best suit. But it isn't, and neither are humans. Constantly yearning for something or someone better; playing the game of "if only" as in, "If only he weren't bald/she could lose five pounds," is tantamount to yearning for the shining knight who whisks you up onto his white steed. It happens only in fairy tales. Deal with what is.

90

It's not all the other guy's fault

People in relationships mirror each other. Psychologists say that whatever's bugging one half of a couple is bound to be a quality of the other partner, too. That's why the things that bug us so much bug us so much—they're things that, deep down, we don't like about ourselves. If your honey is drinking too much, ask yourself in what way or what area of your life you're trying to escape. If she's lounging around all the time doing nothing, where in your life are you not taking responsibility? The answers are always interesting.

91

Where will you be . . .

. . . five years from now? Experts say people with a five-year plan are the most effective at reaching their goals. Ten years is too long; one year is too short. It's good to have a plan; otherwise, couples can drift along and become prey to the "this isn't going anywhere" pitfall. Even discussing where you want to be in five years' time can reveal fascinating nuggets about your partner you never knew about. And, if you're both clear about what you want to achieve, as individuals as well as a pair, you can help each other get there. Write your plan down and pin it someplace where you can both refer to it. It's easy to lose track.

92

Have a vision

Not the same as a plan, but just as important, is a vision. The happiest couples have a shared vision of what they want in and from a relationship. Talking about your vision is hugely revealing. You might want children and a big house in the country, but he dreams of an urban loft and a dog. Or maybe his vision involves a relationship that helps him do more work, while you want hearts and flowers all the way. Again, you might have to adjust your visions so they meet halfway. Clarifying a vision can help clarify many of the unspoken expectations we carry around in that file in our heads marked "love."

A fun exercise to do together is to draw your vision. You don't need to be artists, but a colorful picture of your vision is a great thing to have. And it's more likely to make it happen, say visualization experts.

93

Don't live in each other's pockets

There's always some truth in a cliché, and "familiarity breeds contempt" is a cliché for a reason. Yes, familiarity also breeds intimacy, but if you live in each other's pockets and don't do anything outside the relationship, you'll have nothing fresh to bring to it. Creating a balance between togetherness and separateness, intimacy and solitude, is one of the trickiest tasks committed couples face, in part because the amount of alone-time and space we all need changes constantly. Give each other time and space; talk about how much time alone, with each other, and with friends you each need, and honor your differences.

Feeling needy? Telling him you want him around a lot right now is much better than picking a fight about how much he's going out. Plus, it gives the poor man a chance to *understand*.

94

Don't lose yourself

Some people forget that a relationship is a meeting of two individuals. When the love of his life says she hates football, he gives up the sport he loves. When her sweetheart says he believes in a left-wing agenda, she might switch her politics. But you'll never get your needs met if you put yourself second and don't speak up for your needs, your desires, your beliefs. And you'll never get the chance to find out if your lover loves you for who you really are. Women, especially, are bad at saying no because they fear abandonment if they disagree or if they dislike. But living someone else's life and not yours, however much you love that person, will only make you unhappy.

95

What do you believe in?

Our relationship beliefs lie at the core of our attitude to love. We absorb these beliefs from our parents, our teachers, and role models of relationships around us when we were growing up. Negative beliefs—"All men are stupid," "All women are crazy," "Sex is dirty," "Love never lasts"—are not helpful when you're trying to create a lifetime love. Positive ones—"A loving relationship takes work," "You must treat your partner with respect," "Sex is wonderful"—obviously don't get in the way.

Once you uncover these beliefs and see them for what they are, you stand a chance of changing them. If you come up against some negative beliefs, you do have to consciously think, "Hang on, I don't want to believe that anymore." Then behave like you don't believe it and choose a different belief.

96

Remember the good stuff

Never stop being romantic about anniversaries and birthdays. Leave each other little love notes, love texts, love messages. Never forget it's a miracle that, out of all the people in the world, you found and fell in love with one who happens to love you back.

97

How are you?

It really is true that you need to be happy with yourself to be happy with someone else. That's why people who've made a good job of being single often make the best partners. Don't expect your partner to *make* you happy. That way disappointment lies. Your partner should be a happy appendage to a happy you. Be the person you want to be with.

Nothing stays the same

Your relationship, if it's a good one, will change enormously over time. It will change if one of you gets a new job, if you move, if you have children. A happy relationship is a living, evolving thing. But relationships do go through what some couples experts call the dead zone, periods when everything feels the same-old, same-old. Even so, if just one of you does something different, the whole relationship will evolve once again. Never try to stay static.

Relationships do take work

You hear it over and over: "Relationships take work." Well, what kind of work? And how? The answer is the kind of work that feels incredibly painful, that brings up all your hopes and fears and exposes all the difficult stuff in your psychological closet. The sort that has you living with boredom, and dislike, and disappointment, and raging fury, and still managing to slap a loving smile on your face occasionally. One of the reasons relationships can feel so challenging, according to marital therapist Dr. Harville Hendrix, is that we tend to attract partners who reflect the positive *and* negative aspects of both our parents.

We don't do it consciously, of course. In his book *Getting The Love You Want* (Pocket Books), Hendrix acknowledges that we may have deliberately searched for people who were radically different from our caretakers. "But, no matter what their conscious intentions, most people are attracted to mates who have their caretakers' positive and

negative traits, and, typically, the negative traits are more influential."
And then we tend to respond in the worst ways our parents did.

Hendrix suggests we do this in an attempt to heal our deepest
psychological wounds—and we all have some. Healing all this when it
does come up is one of the reasons a committed, loving relationship
can do more for you than years of therapy. What Hendrix calls the
"conscious marriage" is "a state of mind and a way of being based on
acceptance, a willingness to grow and change, the courage to
encounter ones own fear, and a conscious decision to act in loving
ways." Result? Happiness.

100

Commitment

A loving, long-term relationship, whether it involves marriage or not, does require commitment. Some people forget that. It takes commitment to talk through difficult things when you're not feeling especially loving. It takes commitment not to respond when the cutest person in the office is flirting with you and your partner has been ignoring you for, like forever. If you've had trouble committing to relationships in the past, think about where in your life you *are* committed, and try to bring those qualities to your love life. It's not easy, but it's worth it. As the philosopher Goethe said, "Commitment has magic in it. Begin it. Now."

Relationships guru Chuck Spezzano says that when things get tricky, true commitment is about "making the other person more important than your problems." If you can manage that, your partner is fortunate indeed. Good luck!

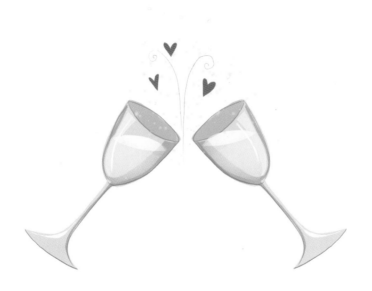